St. Patrick's Day Riddles

and
Trick Questions
for Kids & Family!

Puzzling Riddles & Brain Teasers that Kids and Family will Enjoy

With
Fun Illustrations

Riddleland

Table of Contents

Riddleland Bonus Book

Join our **Facebook Group** at **Riddleland for Kids** to get daily jokes and riddles.

Bonus Book

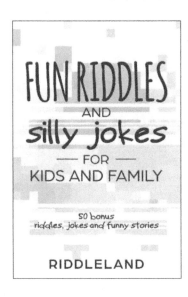

https://pixelfy.me/riddlelandbonus

Thank you for buying this book. As a token of our appreciation, we would like to offer a special bonus—a collection of 50 original jokes, riddles, and funny stories.

Introduction

"May your blessings outnumber the shamrocks that grow. And may trouble avoid you wherever you go"
~ Irish Blessing

We would like to personally thank you for purchasing this book. **St Patrick Riddles and Trick Questions for Kids and Family** book is a collection of fun brain teasers and riddles of easy to hard difficulty.

These brain teasers will challenge children and their parents to think and stretch their minds. They have also many other benefits such as:

• **Bonding** – It is an excellent way for parents and their children to spend some quality time and create some fun and memorable memories.

• **Confidence Building** - When parents ask the riddles, it creates a safe environment for children to burst out answers even if they are incorrect. This helps children to develop self-confidence in expressing themselves.

• **Improve Vocabulary** – Riddles are usually written in advanced words, therefore children will need to understand these words before they can share the riddles.

• **Better reading comprehension** – Many children can read at a young age but may not understand the context of the sentences. Riddles can help develop the children's interest to comprehend the context before they can share it with their friends.

• **Sense of humor** – Funny creative riddles can help children develop their sense of humor while getting their brains working.

Chapter 1

Easy Riddles

"The best luck of all is the luck you make for yourself"

~ Douglas MacArthur

Chapter 1 - Questions

1. As a leprechaun, I consider myself to be frugal. I saved and saved to get the gold I have today. Many other people, though, prefer to use this term to describe me, saying I am a hoarder, selfish, cunning, deviant, and evil. When other people hear this term, they think I am a miner because the two terms are so close, but I got most of my gold through shoe making, tricking humans, and stealing other people's treasure. What is this term people call me?

2. Because leprechauns are outside most of the time, they tend to wear clothes of my color so they can blend in with the leaves and the lawn. The clothes work too well perhaps, because nowadays people question if leprechauns really do exist.

What color am I?

3. I'm all about one country, and yet people everywhere celebrate me.

What am I?

4. We're the biggest English-speaking heritage in the United States, but we're not English. In fact, we'd get pretty mad if you told us we're English!

Who are we?

5. We're of the same mother with our brethren, but we don't follow the same rules and our homes have different names. Our family name is the same, but our brethren's starts with N, and ours with R.

Who are we?

6. You'll find me at the end of a half-circle in all the colors of the world, and while many have seen the path, nobody has ever found me.

What am I?

7. I am the faith to which St. Patrick sought to convert the pagan Irish. My name means "little Christ". I was begun by Jesus of Nazareth. My first great missionary was Paul of Tarsus, but, unlike St. Patrick, St. Paul never made it to Ireland.

What am I?

8. I'm like your dad's favorite place to hang out with his friends. Across the Pond, I'm raised, but back home, I'm short form for a larger name.

What am I?

Chapter 1 - Questions

9. I'm not a genie and I don't come from a lamp. Nobody has seen me, and yet I am not a scam. Although I'm pretty magic, I have no wand. And yet if you find me, three wishes I'll grant.

Who am I?

10. Which letter of the alphabet is closer to Ireland's Cliffs of Moher?

11. I'm like the hat from whence the rabbit came, but I like different clothes and people only wear me one day a year at festivals.

Who am I?

12. We're yellow and we jingle, but in the modern world's values we don't actually mingle. And yet if you have us, you can have any toy without fuss.

What are we?

13. We're like the Turkish shoes you see in Aladdin, but we come from a much colder country. We look great alongside green. We look upwards, and yet we're always down to earth.

What are we?

14. You'll see me on many heads in Ireland, but around the world, I'm pretty rare, for I am a game of chance and genetic flair.

What am I?

15. Tick-tock, I have a golden pot, a red beard, and a green frock but the best part of finding me is?

16. What goes up in an Irish spring, but never moves?

17. I'm a Christian saint, but when my birthday comes, people roam the streets wearing the clothes of a mythical creature.

Who am I?

18. Leprechauns are known for collecting things and for hoarding. I am the most valuable thing they collect. They normally put me in a large black pot so that I don't get lost.

What am I?

Chapter 1 - Questions

19. I have eyes but I cannot see. I am an important Irish vegetable today, but I am not a native of Ireland. I am the root of the Solanum tuberosum plant. I can be found throughout the world. When I was in short supply in Ireland in 1845-1849, a lot of people left Ireland and came to the United States.

What am I?

20. I'm caught between the month of love and the month of Easter, but I'm neither fully winter, nor fully spring.

What am I?

21. What is the largest of its kind in Ireland, runs, but never walks, has a head but it doesn't weep and has a mouth, but it does not speak?

22. What doesn't belong in this list? Shamrock, leprechaun, St. Patrick's Day, tartan, the Cliffs of Moher.

23. You'll see me in green shades on one day of the year. I usually get bigger when I am full, and if you don't tie me down, I will fly away (but I have no wings).

What am I?

24. Why is it that all those who have found the leprechaun, always found him in the last place they looked for him?

25. Although my name may make you think of seething with impatience, I am an Irish dish consisting of lamb, potatoes, onions, and carrots. Different cooks, however, may vary the recipe; for instance, some substitute goat for the lamb; others leave out the carrots.

What am I?

26. Leprechauns usually keep their gold hidden underground where no one can see it, but when they do bring it outside to admire it, I am the spot that leprechauns like to keep their gold. For humans to see me, it must first rain.

What am I?

27. Because many of them are cobblers, leprechauns can be seen running around wearing me. I am also seen in the kitchen or in the barbeque pit; I am designed to protect your fancy clothing from stains and rips. I sometimes have pockets so that leprechauns can put nails in me; I may even have a loop for them to store their hammer.

What am I?

Chapter 1 - Questions

28. Although some leprechauns are known for mining, most are engaged in my profession. People in my field are interested in soles, but not souls like St. Patrick was interested in. They are interested in tongues, but not the gossiping tongues like St. Patrick was interested in. Before you criticize a leprechaun and his profession, walk a mile in his shoes.

What is my profession?

29. The following can all be said to belong to a type of mythical creature?: leprechaun, Tinker-Bell, Godmother, Puck. Can you guess what it is?

30. The leprechaun is up to no good again; he took some words and scrambled them! Unscramble these words to make them rhyme: rshmaock and lriakco.

31. Superstition says there are a lot of ways to get me into your life - blow out all your birthday candles, carry a rabbit's foot, cross your fingers, or find a four leaf-clover.

What am I?

32. I don't grow tall, sometimes I have three hands, sometimes four, I'm green but no alien, who am I then?

FUN FACT

Do you know what is the highest number of leaves to ever be found on a clover? It's a whopping 14!!!!

Chapter 1 - Questions

33. As a leprechaun, I have four forms of magic. One, I have great strength for my size; I can even overpower humans. Two, I know how to grant wishes and cast spells. Three, I have the power of regeneration; I can regrow missing body parts. I also have a fourth power; this power enables me to escape to safety in most cases and to reach a pot of gold before anyone else. What is my fourth power?

34. What will you find in Ireland, but not in shamrock?

35. Leprechauns are known for living in one of two places; one place is underground in a hole and I am the other place. I am the leprechaun's branch office if you'll pardon the pun. I am the home to some other squirrely creatures as well.

What am I?

36. What does St. Patrick's have in common with all the weeks?

37. I am the city that hosted the first recorded St. Patrick's Day parade. I am in the United States. I've hosted other big events too; immediately prior to the American Revolution, I hosted a famous tea party. The professional basketball team in my town also celebrates the city's Irish heritage.

What is my name?

38. I have six eyes, but I cannot see; I have a tongue, but I cannot speak. I have a sole, but I do not live. I may have been touched by leprechaun hands.

What am I?

39. Just as humans want to capture leprechauns, leprechauns want to capture humans. I am the bait that the leprechauns use to attract humans. My name is a color; I am often associated with first place. If your downfall is greed, I will be very appealing to you, but when you come to get me the mischievous leprechaun may come to get you.

What am I?

40. I am a number between one and ten. The term "leprechaun" means "small body." If a leprechaun is my height in feet, the leprechaun is considered tall. I am also the number of leaves on a shamrock. What is my name?

41. Leprechauns wear me on their shoes for decorations instead of around their pants to keep their pants from falling.

What am I?

42. The leprechaun is measuring his gold, but he can't count all the coins. He is about three feet tall and wears a proper size 5 in shoes. What does he weigh?

43. The shamrock is one plant, but it has three leaves. St. Patrick stressed these three-distinct-beings and yet still one-being when describing me. He said that God was the overall plant, but Father, Son, and Holy Ghost were the leaves. What do I represent?

Chapter 1 - Questions

44. St. Patrick was not the first missionary to Ireland, but he was the most influential. What was to become known as the Celtic cross, though, was present long before these missionaries came along. The cross represented the elements of the planet - earth, wind, fire, and me. You can drink me, swim in me, and bathe in me. What element am I?

45. Leprechauns are known for playing a variety of instruments, including the flute, the fiddle, and me. I am a woodwind instrument with reed pipes that are fed with a constant reservoir of air which is forced through a bag by the musician's arm. What is my name?

46. St. Patrick was not the birth name of the man who Christianized Ireland. In fact, "Saint" was a title bestowed upon the bishop following his death. "Patrick" was a name the person selected for himself. The name has the same root as "patriarch". The term refers to this missionary being a priest, being a nurturer, and being a leader. What is the English translation of "Patrick?"

Chapter 1 - Questions

47. Aside from the leprechaun's treasure, this is the only thing related to him that will always increase and never decrease.

What is it?

48. Leprechauns are all of one gender - me! Although I am the name of a gender, my name makes them sound as if the leprechauns were letter carriers, although most work as cobblers.

What am I?

49. I am the number of leprechauns that you are likely to find in any given hole. Leprechauns tend to stay to themselves, playing their own jig music and dancing to it. Although leprechauns have social skills and can hold conversations, most prefer to stay to themselves. What number am I?

50. I am the name of the hat that the typical leprechaun wears. You can also call me a derby, bombin, bobby cock, bob hat. Although I am a hard felt hat with a rounded crown, my name sounds as if I might play ten-pins at the local bowling alley. What is my name?

51. The Irish flag has three colors in three equal-sized vertical columns. The first column is green and represents nationalism and Irish Catholicism. The third color is orange and represents Irish Protestants. The color between the Catholic green and the Protestant orange is me, white. What do I represent?

52. I am the bait you would want to use to capture a leprechaun. Just as mice crave cheese, leprechauns crave me. Just as mice lose self-control around cheese and make bad decisions resulting in getting trapped, when a leprechaun is around me the leprechaun does not use common sense and will fall for a trap.

What am I?

53. Aside from coin-counting, what is the leprechaun's favorite subject?

54. The pagans not only used the Celtic cross to remember the four elements, but they also used it to represent four directions as points on a compass - north, south, east, and me. I am the direction in which the sunsets each night. Whereas Celtic people looked forward to the East, they dreaded me, for I often brought dark and bitter cold.

What am I?

55. When you stir sugar and milk into your Irish tea drink, what hand is better to use, what do you think?

56. St. Patrick carried a walking cane made of wood from me. Whenever he stopped, he would poke the walking stick into the ground. One day he talked so long that the stick grew roots. My name sounds like I have been burnt to a crisp; it even rhymes with "trash" - but I am anything but trashy. What kind of tree am I?

57. The term "leprechaun" means "small body", and in some countries small-bodied people/fairies aren't the people who dress in green.I am one of those small-bodied people. I am not a gnome, leprechaun, elf, or dwarf. My name will remind you of a lemon-lime drink like 7-Up.

What am I?

FUN FACT

Do you know how many people in the US have Irish Ancestors? It is 34.7 million, which is more than 7 times the actual population of Ireland!

Ireland •

34.7 million
people in the US
have Irish Ancestors

• United State

Chapter 1 - Questions

58. You get an extra wish from the leprechaun if you guess this one: what is the only thing you will have to break before you can actually use it?

59. I am the name of St. Patrick's nationality. St. Patrick was not originally from Ireland; he was from Wales. (Wales is part of the United Kingdom today. Wales borders England and is otherwise surrounded by water; it has the Irish Sea to its north and west, and the Bristol Channel to the south.) If being from Ireland makes you Irish, what does being from Wales make you?

60. To hold the office of saint, one must have passed on to the next world. One must also have written, and one's teachings needed to line up with Roman Catholic doctrine. As in the case of St. Patrick, one must also have done this - it didn't have to be turning water into wine; getting rid of all the snakes in Ireland or having one's staff blossom into a tree - but those all would count. What must a saint do?

61. I am part of the Trinity. St. Patrick used the shamrock to explain the Trinity to pagans who had trouble grasping that one God could be three gods. Each leaf of the shamrock represented one aspect of God, with all three leaves comprising the plant just as all three aspects of God came together to make God. Although all three branches of the Trinity were equal in St. Patrick's eyes, many consider me to be third rate. My name has changed over the years because people thought Holy Ghost was too scary. What is my name?

62. I am the organ of vision and light sensitivity. Leprechauns are said to move amazingly fast. That's why, if you see one and point it out to your friend, your friend may not see it. People say that leprechauns are as fast as a blink of me.

What am I?

63. Every year on St. Patrick's Day the Chicago River is dyed a Kelly green. I am the number of hours that the river will stay green. I am more than the fingers you have on one hand, and three less than the number of fingers you have on both hands.

What number am I?

64. I am the term used to describe what happened to St. Patrick at the age of 16. My name means "to take someone away illegally", but it sounds as if a child is sleeping.

What am I?

Chapter 1 - Questions

65. St. Patrick earned this religious title. People with this title represent the Church to the world, govern all the Catholics in their jurisdiction, teach doctrine, and perform religious rituals. Supposedly, the person who holds this office has been touched by someone who has been touched by someone who was touched ceremoniously by one of the original Apostles and, by the laying-on-of-hands by a bishop, this special office was given to St. Patrick.

What is it?

66. The first St. Patrick's Day celebration was held in me, the country with the largest Irish population. Believe it or not, that country is not Ireland. Ireland may have the most Irish citizens, but I have the most people with an Irish ancestry. Today a statue stands in the harbor of the town that hosted this celebration; that statue welcomes immigrants. Which country am I?

67. The leprechaun's going to grant you three wishes, but first, you have to spell that without any S's. How do you do it?

68. Is the little green king of mischief telling the truth or is it fluff? He says he found an old coin in his pot, dated 150 B.C. - is that the truth or a lie, what can you see?

Chapter 1 - Questions

69. Did you know boxing is the sport that made the Irish most famous in the Olympics? What if the leprechaun told you that, during a match, one of the players got knocked out by being punched after just three rounds, and yet, no man threw a punch? What do you think?

70. You know how some people wake up all happy when they get out of bed? Leprechauns don't! I am the word that is used to describe the typical leprechaun's typical mood. Their moods may make you irritable too, so it's appropriate that I rhyme with "ouch-y". How are their moods best described?

Chapter 1 - Questions

71. Almost everybody knows that the fourth leaf on a four-leaf clover represents luck. What they don't know is what I, the second leaf, represents. The first leaf represents faith. The third leaf presents hope. In a letter to the Corinthians, St. Paul, who heavily influenced St. Patrick, said that life required faith, hope, and me, and that I was greater than faith or hope. What do I, the second leaf of the three-leaf clover - or the four-leaf clover for that matter, represent?

 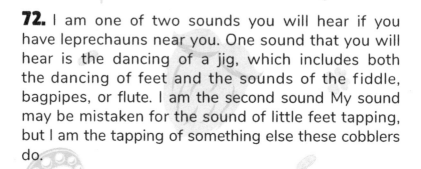

72. I am one of two sounds you will hear if you have leprechauns near you. One sound that you will hear is the dancing of a jig, which includes both the dancing of feet and the sounds of the fiddle, bagpipes, or flute. I am the second sound My sound may be mistaken for the sound of little feet tapping, but I am the tapping of something else these cobblers do.

What am I?

73. Leprechauns are hard to spot in me because they wear green. They live in meadows and around me, and therefore the green works as camouflage. I have a trunk, but I have no arms or legs. I am known for my acorns, and squirrels find me a bit nutty.

What am I?

FUN FACT

Do you know how likely you are to find a four-leaf clover? The odds of finding one, are approximately 1 in every 10,000 clovers.

74. The leprechaun wants to do some crazy maths! He's thinking of a number of coins (smaller than 100). If he reverses its digits, it will increase its value by one-fifth. What is the number of coins the leprechaun has in mind?

---

75. I am what leprechauns do with their gold coins. My name means "to store up for future use". I am the opposite of spend.

What is my name?

---

76. I am the day and month that St. Patrick passed from this world to the next. It is on this day each year that St. Patrick's Day is celebrated.

What day am I?

---

77. Sometimes you can tell that a leprechaun is nearby due to the smell. Leprechauns do not have a strong body odor, but they do have one vile, smelly habit they have not broken. When you get close to a leprechaun, what do you smell?

---

78. St. Patrick was in Ireland as a slave for ten years before escaping to Great Britain. He returned to Ireland in my year as a Christian missionary. If you say the individual numerals of my year it sounds like a countdown to "one".

What year am I?

79. I am the name for the mound of dirt that magically appears in a lawn. As Leprechauns dig their home underground, all of that dirt must go somewhere; in many cases, the leprechauns pile it in one central location, much like you would pile dirt if you were digging a basement. In other cases, I am simply a slight hill the leprechaun makes as he journeys through the soil. Although some people blame this dirt on moles or other animals, other people have reported seeing leprechauns near me. In fact, I am considered proof by many that a leprechaun is living in the area. If the woodland animals were to play a game of baseball, I would be where the pitcher stands to throw. What is my name?

80. A pound of shamrock is the same as a pound of gold - is this true, or is it too bold?

Chapter 1 - Answers

1. Miser

2. Green.

3. St. Patrick's Day, which is celebrated all over the world by people of Irish heritage and not only! In fact, many people claim to be "Irish for a Day" just to take in the fun of this celebration!

4. The Irish

5. The Republic of Ireland, which is separated from Northern Ireland and independent from the United Kingdom (unlike Northern Ireland, which is part of the United Kingdom and subject to the Queen of England).

6. The pot of gold at the end of the rainbow

7. Christianity.

8. A pub, which is like a bar, but in America (hence, the "raising the bar" suggestion)

9. A leprechaun, which is a character in Irish folklore who will grant you three wishes if you find him.

10. C (sea), as the Cliffs of Moher, are on a beach.

11. A green hat frequently associated with both leprechauns and St. Patrick's Day.

12. Golden coins. Although not used as currency in the modern world, golden coins are as valuable as the amount of gold in them.

13. The leprechaun's shoes, with their pointy shape (which might seem similar to those of the traditional Turkish costume).

14. Red hair. Although extremely common in Ireland, red hair is considered to be one of the least common genes in the world.

15. You get three wishes that come true when you find a leprechaun.

16. The temperature!

17. St. Patrick, who is considered to be the Patron Saint of Ireland, and also the one who brought Christianity to Ireland. On St. Patrick's Day, many people dress up as leprechauns,

Chapter 1 - Answers

though, which is a mythical creature in the Irish folklore.

18. Gold coins.

19. Potato

20. March, the month of St. Patrick's Day (which falls on March 17th

21. River Shannon (the largest/ longest river in Ireland).

22. Tartan (which is a traditional Scottish fabric, not Irish).

23. A green balloon.

24. Because once you find him you stop looking, and that is the last place you looked.

25. Irish stew

26. The end of the rainbow.

---

27. Apron.

28. Shoe cobbler.

29. Fairies

30. Shamrock and Airlock

31. Good luck.

32. A clover

33. Super speed.

34. Letters "I", "E", "N", "L" and "D".

35. A hollow tree.

36. "DAY" (because you have St Patrick's day and Monday, Tuesday, Wednesday, Thursday, Friday, Saturday, and Sunday).

37. Boston. The Boston Tea Party was in 1775; the Boston Celtics are the National Basketball League's professional team in Boston.

38. A shoe.

---

39. Gold.

40. The numeral three

41. Buckle.

42. The coins (since he cannot count them).

43. The Holy Trinity

44. Water.

45. Bagpipes.

46. Father figure.

47. His age

48. Male man.

49. The number one.

50. Bowler.

51. Peace and harmony between the two groups

52. Gold coin.

33

Chapter 1 - Answers

53. Spelling (because the leprechaun can cast spells).

54. West.

55. Neither, you will want to use a spoon, not a hand.

56. Ash.

57. Sprite.

58. An egg

59. Welsh

60. Perform a miracle

61. Holy Spirit

62. An eye

63. Five; thumbs are not fingers.

64. Kidnap.

65. Bishop.

---

66. United States; the first St. Patrick's Day celebration was in New York City in 1762.

67. "T-H-A-T".

68. He is lying, a coin cannot be dated with "BC" because during "BC times", people did not have the notion of "BC".

69. No man threw a punch, but this might have been a women's match!

70. Grouchy.

71. Love.

72. The tap, tap, tapping of a hammer.

73. Oak Tree

74. 46

75. Save.

---

76. March 17. St. Patrick passed away on March 17, 461.

77. The smoke from his pipe.

78. 432.

79. Fairy mound.

80. Yes, they are both one pound.

Chapter 2

Hard Riddles

"St Patrick's Day is an enchanted time – a day to begin transforming winter's dreams into summer's magic."

~ Adrienne Cook

1. Many people in Ireland come in my color. If you feed me, I will grow. If you give me water, though, I will die.

What am I?

2. I'm a main city in Ireland, and here Ulysses was written. It's not the Greek one, but a modern take on it. I am the city of... ?

3. I'm a place that's beautiful in French, and pretty speedy in English. What's my name?

4. Can you think of something green that is served, but never eaten?

5. I'm quite frail and I grow on the ground. At first, I look like a scam, but then, in the end, I'm pretty sturdy.

What am I?

6. A gold coin is certainly important if you want to catch a leprechaun, but I am important too. I provide the light that strikes the gold coin; this gleam makes the leprechaun aware that the coin is there, for coins don't have a smell to them.

What am I?

Chapter 2 - Questions

7. I'm the master of the green mischief, and although people have talked about me for centuries, they have yet to find my gold stuff.

Who am I?

---

8. The leprechaun's farm has 25 cows and twenty-eight chicken. How many cows didn't eat the chickens?

---

9. You cannot drink me as a kid, but your dad I cannot forbid, a pint or two of my black drink.

What am I?

Hint: the book of World Records and I have something in common, but only in name.

---

10. We often hide the leprechaun's rainbow, we can fly but we don't have wings, we can cry but we do not have eyes. Even more, wherever we go, darkness can follow.

What are we?

---

11. I'm made from an ingredient that sounds like a blooming plant and another ingredient that grows in the land. People around the world eat me, but I am most popular with the Irish and I always will be.

What am I?

---

12. How many letters are there in the Gaelic alphabet?

FUN FACT

Do you know what is the most
common drink consumed
on St. Patrick's Day?
It's beer!

Chapter 2 - Questions

13. Just like nobody has ever found the pot at the end of the rainbow, nobody can answer "yes" to this question.

What is the question?

14. If you toss a pound of golden coins, a pound of shamrock, and a pound of sticks from the Cliffs of Moher downhill, which one will get to the ground the soonest?

15. Which is the most recent year in which St. Patrick's Day preceded New Year's?

16. "Patrick" is a name I decided to call myself, and after I received sainthood, I became known as St. Patrick. My first name sounds as if we might win; my last name sounds like what you do when you put a lollipop in your mouth.

Who am I?

17. If three pots of gold together add up to 30, if two leprechauns and a pot of gold add up to 28 if you subtract a shamrock out of a leprechaun and you get two, then what is the value of a pot of gold, a shamrock, and a leprechaun?

18. What is the exact middle of Ireland?

19. Carrauntoohil is the highest mountain in Ireland. Before they measured it, what was the highest mountain in Ireland?

20. Imagine that you are on a quest to find the pot at the end of the rainbow. To get there, you must first exit a castle room inside of which water is pouring down from the ceiling and the walls are getting closer and closer to each other. How do you get out of this situation?

21. Leprechaun lore began with Celtic culture. The Celts were found in England, Ireland, and me. I contain cave drawings that Celts likely made. I am a continental European country; my capital is Paris.

Where am I?

Chapter 2 - Questions

22. If the leprechaun says, "all leprechauns are liars", is he lying?

23. You had a total of 40 clover leaves. Three of them went into the shamrock you gave your mom. You then gave three four-leaf clovers to your best friend. How many clover leaves are you left with?

24. The leprechaun's counting his money again! To his surprise, he found 8,549,176,320 coins in one pot of gold. Why is this number so unique?

25. How many inches does a foot have for a leprechaun?

26. The leprechaun gives you three coins. As you turn the first one heads up, say, "Mary's mother has three daughters." As you turn the second one heads up, say, "One of them is called Sarah." As you turn the third one heads up, say, "The second one is called Anne." What is the third girl's name?

27. If the leprechaun has 25 coins in his pocket, how many times can he subtract 5 out of them?

28. The leprechaun went to sleep and lit 5 candles. Since he left the window open, the wind blew in and extinguished two of the candles. How many candles will the leprechaun have in the end?

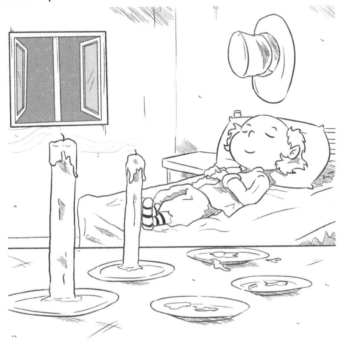

29. Every year a designated fairy gives the leprechaun a gift of a gold coin. The fairy does not visit all leprechauns on the same day but visits a few each day. How can this be that there is "a" special day and yet the fairy makes deliveries year-long?

30. I have chords, but you don't need anything sharp to play me. You won't find me in a regular rock band, but I do appear on stage quite a lot.

What am I?

Chapter 2 - Questions

31. If six leprechauns dig six holes in six hours, how long will it take one leprechaun to dig half a hole for his flower?

---

32. It is known that St. Patrick banished the snakes from Ireland - but if they stayed and went to school, what would be their favorite part of the day?

---

33. I am the name of the high-ranking class in ancient Ireland as well as the name of a religion. In addition to priests, my class included doctors and lawyers. My name means "knowledge of the oak", and I feature a lot of nature worship. Although my members were quite literate, we did not write about our religion; you know of our religion from what other people, such as St. Patrick, have had to say about it. We competed for the hearts and minds with the people, and, like the snakes, St. Patrick drove most of our religion out of Ireland. What are we called?

---

34. Not every leprechaun has a fiddle; some may have bagpipes, flutes, or no instrument at all. Not every leprechaun has red hair; some have white hair or have dyed their hair. Not every leprechaun has a beard; most do, but some are too young to grow one. Many leprechauns live in Ireland, but leprechauns can be found world-wide. However, there is one thing that every leprechaun has.

What is that?

35. The leprechaun got an office job, in a tall, 12-story building but didn't enjoy it. One day he jumped out of the window, but he was not hurt at all. He didn't use magic, so how come he was well?

36. The leprechaun is looking at his coins and he realizes that if 7 is turned into a 12 and 11 is turned into 21, 16 would become...?

37. If an emerald stone is worth 10 bucks and the leprechaun has 30 of them in his pocket, how much money worth of emeralds will he have if he drops 1 and loses 2 of them?

Chapter 2 - Questions

38. Find how many coins there are in the leprechaun's pot if the result of this maths problem is equal to that. 4 * 4 * 3 / 4 (3+3) + 4 =?

39. There are three emeralds in the leprechaun's pocket and about 1,000 coins in his magic pot at the end of the rainbow. How much money does the leprechaun have, really?

40. There are two pots of gold in front of you, but only one is the one that's true, the one at the largest distance from you. All you know is that one of them is 10 centimeters away from you and the other one is 10 inches away from you. Which one will you pick?

41. Leprechauns can be found anywhere, even at schools. One day Lucky the Leprechaun was trapped by a student in the corner of the classroom. Lucky offered to give the student anything he wanted; the student wanted to have all his answers be right on the next quiz. Did the trickster grant his wish?

42. Jose bragged that nothing scared him. Therefore, when he caught a leprechaun, he insisted that the leprechaun show him something that would give him pause. The leprechaun did as he was told; what did he give to the boy who feared nothing?

FUN FACT

Do you know how short the shortest St. Patrick's Day Parade was? It was just 77 feet. This was in Dripsey in County Cork, Ireland, between 2 pubs: the Weigh Inn and the Lee Valley.

Weigh Inn
- Pub -

77 feet

Lee Valley
- Pub -

Chapter 2 - Questions

43. The leprechaun has 1,000 coins and adds 40 to them. Then, he adds another 1,000, then 30, then 1,000, then 20, then 1,000, and then, for the last time, 10. How many coins does the leprechaun have now?

44. Would you like a fourth wish, now that you have met the king of mischief? Solve this and he will grant it for you: Sean is two years old and Mary, his sister, is half as old as him. When Sean will be 100, how old will Mary be?

45. The leprechaun wants to find a new hiding spot for three of his pots of gold. He assigns a number to each of them, from one to ten, which coincidentally is also how many coins there are in each respective pot. He will only hideaway those that is a prime number. How many coins will the leprechaun hide?

46. Mary, John, and Sean decided that they want to surprise their parents with some cute, homemade gifts for St. Patrick's Day. Mary spent about half of what John spent on these presents, and Sean spent three times more than Mary. In total, they spent $720. How much money did each of them spend?

47. The leprechaun's lied all this time! It looks like the pot of gold is not at the end of a rainbow, but in a place, the little fairy describes as "the only place where, if you take more out of it, it becomes bigger". What is this place?

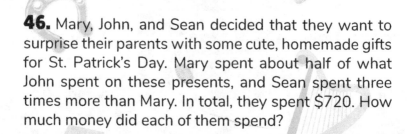

Chapter 2 - Questions

48. If you want to guess how many coins the leprechaun has in one pot, think of the next number in this series: 112, 119, 126, 133, 140...?

49. Susie caught a leprechaun. As leprechauns are prone to do, he introduced himself – "Hi, I'm Lucky" – and offered to grant a wish in exchange for his freedom. Believing she could have all the leprechaun magic, Susie said, "I wish I were you." The leprechaun, a trickster, said, "Very well. Enjoy your new name," and then he ran away. Susie wondered what her new name was, and then it dawned on her that she had been tricked. What was Susie's new name?

50. The leprechaun is keeping up with the times and he has just bought his mobile phone! He wants to multiply all the numbers on it but doesn't know the answer. Can you work out the answer?

51. The leprechaun wants to collect 1,000 coins, but he only wants them in stashes of 8. How will you add them up to make up the sum?

52. You know the trick already: if you answer this, you'll get another wish come true from your leprechaun! What do the numbers 88, 69, and 11 have in common?

Chapter 2 - Questions

53. Mrs. Flannigan had three pies and two cobblers on her kitchen countertop. She put the pies in the oven, but she let the cobblers stay on the counter top. When her husband came home and looked into the oven, her husband noticed there was room in the oven for the cobblers as well as the pies. Why did she leave the cobblers on the counter?

54. I am a sheet of metal. I am as thin as paper, and I am sometimes used to wrap chocolate coins people give on St. Patrick's Day. Although I come in a variety of colors, I am usually gold. To the leprechaun I pass as real gold, and when I cover a chocolate coin, leprechauns think the whole coin is solid gold. Because leprechauns have a hard time telling real gold coins from fake chocolate coins; many of your chocolate candies may disappear at night.

What am I?

55. A pot of shamrock and a leprechaun hat cost $140 in total. We know the leprechaun hat is $100 more than the pot of shamrock. How much does each of the items cost?

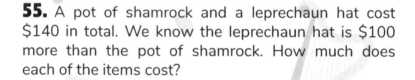

56. When the most recently born leprechaun was just 31 years old, I was 8 years old. Now his age is twice mine. How old am I now?

Chapter 2 - Questions

57. The leprechaun has two pots with him. The first one contains just emerald stones and the second one contains just golden coins. The two pots have an equal number of precious items in them. How can the leprechaun arrange them to boost the chances of grabbing an emerald stone from each of the buckets (if he doesn't look?)

58. If you solve the following equation, you will get the year in which St. Patrick is believed to have been born: 100*4-100+4*2+6

Chapter 2 - Questions

59. Kelly Green is perceived as the most beautiful color by most Irish. Before Kelly Green was discovered, what was the most beautiful color?

60. Frank wanted to be a basketball player, so, when he caught a leprechaun and got offered a wish, he wished, "I want to be taller than my dad." The leprechaun said he granted the wish, but Frank didn't feel any taller. Upon inspection, though, Frank was taller than his dad. How could this be?

61. Your St. Patrick's Day party has seven guests, all men. Each of them will shake hands only once with each of the other men. How many handshakes will take place?

62. One day while Kelsey was playing in a field, he came across a leprechaun. The leprechaun saw easy money to be made, so he held out a gold coin and said, "I will bet you a gold coin that I am faster than a flash." Kelsey said, "No way," and accepted his deal. The leprechaun ran and proved he was faster than the speed of light. Not to be outdone Kelsey said, "Big deal. See that house over there? I can jump higher than it." The leprechaun laughed, "No way." They agreed that Kelsey could have his gold coin back if he jumped higher than the house. Was Kelsey exaggerating or telling the truth?

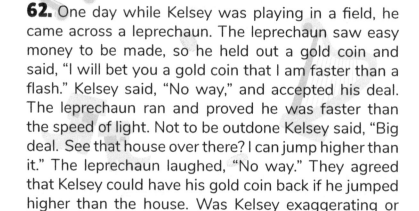

63. Sean's mother had three sons. One of them was called February, the other one April, and the third one was born on the 17th of March. What was the name of the third son?

64. Your parents have a lot of books about Ireland and St. Patrick's Day, but you never knew exactly how many. If you take a book out of the bookshelf, the sixth from the right and the 4th one from the left, can you guess the number of books your parents have on this topic?

Chapter 2 - Questions

65. Sally was looking through the family photo album with her grandpa and saw a picture of her dad in 1987 as a middle-class child looking up and pointing excitedly at a rainbow. Grandpa said dad ran into the house that day to tell Grandma where they were going to follow it, and then they started to run after the rainbow. Why did her dad make the trip back to the house to talk to his mom in person instead of using a cellphone to call?

66. What letter of the alphabet lies between Great Britain and Ireland?

67. Let's say that you spot a red-headed full-bearded leprechaun in a field. He does not look childish, but he has no white hair. He is busy playing the fiddle and dances a jig with ease. With just this information, you should be able to tell how many birthdays he has had. Therefore, I will ask you, how many birthdays has the leprechaun had?

68. There is a very large St. Patrick's party going on and 100 people are invited. If 85 of the guests have a green bag, 75 of them are wearing leprechaun hats, 60 of them come with an umbrella in case it rains in March, and 90 of them wear an all-green outfit, how many of the guests have all these four characteristics?

FUN FACT

Do you know what happens to the shamrocks that are given to the US President by the Irish Leader each St. Patrick's Day? The shamrocks are grown in Kerry, they're presented to the President in a crystal bowl; but then immediately after the exchange they're destroyed by the Secret Service!

Chapter 2 - Answers

1. Fire. Note: Most Irish people have red color hair. Red hair is also sometimes called firey hair.

2. Dublin

3. Belfast (where "belle" means "beautiful" in French and "fast" is a synonym for "speedy")

4. A tennis ball (you serve it in a tennis game, but you will never eat it).

---

5. Shamrock (where "sham" is a synonym of "scam" and "rock" is the "sturdy part").

6. Moon: you are most likely to catch a leprechaun at night. Although leprechauns are around in the day, they prefer to operate under the cover of night because that is when humans typically sleep.

7. A leprechaun frequently associated with mischief and the color green.

---

8. Five. If you say "twenty-eight" out loud, it sounds like "twenty ate" - which means that five cows (out of twenty-five) did not eat chicken. This is an absurd riddle, of course, since cows don't eat chicken anyway - but the key is paying attention to the words and how they sound.

9. Guinness, a popular Irish stout beer (and "Guinness World Records" is also the name of the official book that shows the most impressive records in the world).

Chapter 2 - Answers

10. Clouds

11. Potato bread (made, along with other basic ingredients, with flour, which sounds like "flower", and potatoes, which grow in the "land"). Along with soda bread and wheaten bread, potato bread is one of the most popular types of bread in Ireland.

12. There are fourteen letters in the "Gaelic alphabet".

13. The question is "Are you asleep?"

14. They are equally heavy, so unless the wind is involved, they will reach the ground at approximately the same time.

15. St. Patrick's always comes after New Year's (but since most people start the New Year celebrations on the 31st of December, they also have a feeling it's the last holiday of the year, when, in fact, it is the first).

16. Maewyn Succat; "may win sucker"

17. 26

18. "L" is the exact middle of the word "Ireland".

19. Carrauntoohil was still the highest mountain in Ireland (it's just that they hadn't measured it).

20. You stop imagining (since this is entirely an imaginary situation).

21. France

22. The leprechaun is a mythical creature, so it cannot actually say anything "true" in the full sense of the word.

Chapter 2 - Answers

23. 25

24. All its digits are arranged in alphabetical order.

25. 12 (the same as for everyone else).

26. Mary (it says so in the first statement you make as you turn the first coin).

27. Only once (because once he has subtracted the 5 coins, he won't have 25 anymore).

---

28. Two (the ones that were blown out by the wind, because the other ones "lived" to burn to the end).

29. The birthday fairy gives a gold coin to the leprechaun on his birthday. Leprechauns typically put the coin in their pot for safe keeping; leprechauns live for hundreds of years, so an older leprechaun will have a small fortune within his cauldron.

30. A harp (which is considered to be the national musical instrument of Ireland).

---

31. Can't happen - the second he digs a hole, it's a hole (there is no such thing as a "half-hole").

32. Recesssss, of course

33. Druids.

34. A pot of gold

35. He was on the first floor.

36. 31 (you add increasing multipliers of 5 - first 5, then 10, and then 15).

Chapter 2 - Answers

37. 280 (he only loses two of them, the third one is just dropped, so he can retrieve it and account for it).

38. 76

39. None, he has valuable items, but no actual currency/ money per se.

40. 10 inches is approximately 25 centimeters, so the pot at 10 inches is the one that is farthest away from you.

---

41. Of course it was granted and "Right" was given to the answer to every question on his answer sheet; it's a shame none of the questions asked "What is the opposite of left?" or "What is the opposite of wrong?"

42. A dog; the dog was quite willing to shake hands with both front paws.

43. 4,100 (many will be tempted to say "5,000" here, but the correct answer is 4,100).

---

44. 99.

45. 2+3+5+7=17

46. $120, $240, and $360.

47. A hole

48. 147 (you just add 7 to each subsequent number).

49. Sisie.

50. 0 (because zero multiplied by any other number is always zero).

Chapter 2 - Answers

51. 8+8+8+88+888.

52. They show the same number when they are turned upside down.

53. The cobblers were leprechauns who made shoes; they were not pastry treats - she did not want to hurt them.

54. Foil.

55. The pot of shamrock costs $20 and the leprechaun hat costs $120.

56. 23

---

57. He should keep just one emerald stone in one pot and mix the rest of the emerald stones and the coins in the other pot.

58. 386

59. Kelly Green; just because it wasn't discovered doesn't mean it didn't exist.

60. The leprechaun had shrunk Frank's dad to be smaller than Frank.

61. 40.

62. Telling the truth; houses can't jump.

63. Sean (It's in the statement)

---

64. 9 (6+4)-1 = 89

65. The general population didn't have cellphones at that time; cellphones became a middle-class fixture between 1990-1995.

66. "C" (sea). The Celtic Sea lies between the island of Ireland and the island of Great Britain.

67. Just one; he was only born once.

68. 10

Chapter

3

Diffcult Riddles

"I've always thought you've got to
believe in luck to get it"

~ Victoria Holt

1. What word is always pronounced wrong by the Irish?

---

2. Mr. Flannigan was a very superstitious Irishman who believed Irish lore. One day he substituted in the elementary school because a teacher was ill. He stepped into the hall for a minute to talk to the principal and, when he came back into the classroom, he noticed his glasses were moved. He asked who had touched them. Knowing Mr. Flannigan believed in leprechauns, the guilty student called, "I saw a female leprechaun run across your desk; she had her red hair in a pixie cut." Was Mr. Flannigan fooled?

---

3. You always wanted to find the leprechaun, and now that you have finally stumbled upon him, you tell him, "Oh, how I wish I found you sooner!" To your surprise though, the leprechaun will only grant you two wishes now.

Why is that?

4. I'm kind of a fairy, but I don't have wings. In fact, I pretty much deal with the art of shoemaking. Secretly, though, I have a fortune I have hidden where nobody else has ever seen it.

Who am I?

5. I sound like a "buzz" in Greek, but I am proud to say: I'm Irish. People here listen to me, but people everywhere have learned to love me.

What am I?

6. What language will an Irish billboard speak?

Chapter 3 - Questions

7. I'm the most precious green you'll ever find, and although you'll find me on the second-largest island on the European continent, most of my folk come from a Spanish-speaking country.

What am I?

---

8. If you solved the previous riddle, you now know how else Ireland is called. What is the other name of this country?

---

9. One island, two countries, divided by history and different armies.

Who am I?

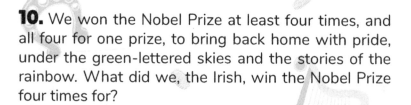

10. We won the Nobel Prize at least four times, and all four for one prize, to bring back home with pride, under the green-lettered skies and the stories of the rainbow. What did we, the Irish, win the Nobel Prize four times for?

---

11. I'm striped, but I'm not wild. I'm strong, but I don't bite. I'm an animal, but only in meaning. Most times, I'm associated with Asians, but this time, it's all about the green pastures of an island.

What am I?

FUN FACT

Do you know who Maewyn Succat is? That's the name that St. Patrick was born with. He changed it to Patricius after he became a priest, and then he became more commonly known as St. Patrick.

Chapter 3 - Questions

12. I am spoken in Ireland, but not in England. I am an official language, and yet fewer and fewer know me.

What am I?

13. What has a rainbow, but can never be found?

14. Where is one place you can always find gold?

Chapter 3 - Questions

15. The Leprechaun finds it easy to get into it, but difficult to get out of.

What is it?

---

16. What has an arch, but starts with a thinking sound?

---

17. What has two eyes but cannot actually see?

---

18. How many letters are there in the Irish language?

19. The first part of our name is similar to that of "vile", and the last part is the spouse of a "queen". Hundreds and hundreds of years ago, we invaded Ireland, but today we're all good friends in Europe.

Who are we?

20. It takes 3 minutes to microwave 3 servings of Irish stew, but how long will it take the leprechaun to microwave twenty-two?

21. Where can you find Northern Ireland and the Republic of Ireland, but no Irish people?

FUN FACT

Did you know that Ireland never had snakes? There is a myth associated with St. Patrick that he stood on top of an Irish hill and banished the snakes from Ireland, but it is thought by researchers that Ireland never had any snakes due to it being surrounded by water, and prior to that covered in ice in a glacial period which was too cold for reptiles.

Chapter 3 - Questions

22. Stan, Virgil, and O'Malley went looking for four-leaf clovers. Stan found twice as many as Virgil. Virgil found half as many as O'Malley. O'Malley didn't find any. How many four-leaf clovers did Stan find?

23. Kelly announced that he no longer believed in leprechauns and that he was not going to go hunting for four-leaf clovers any more. However, your friends say that Kelly was in the field on his knees looking for four-leaf clover yesterday. How could both Kelly and your other friends be telling you the truth?

Chapter 3 - Questions

24. What smells the best at St. Patrick's Day dinner?

25. Leprechauns put all kinds of things in cauldrons, large black pots. For instance, leprechauns typically have one cauldron to put all their gold coins. Sometimes they will make a stew, putting carrots, potatoes, and other ingredients into a cauldron. Although leprechauns put all kinds of things in cauldrons, what is one thing a leprechaun will NEVER put in a cauldron?

26. Bobby traps a leprechaun. In exchange for his freedom, the leprechaun offers to give Bobby three wishes. For his first wish, Bobby says, "I wish I had an extra wish." The leprechaun said okay. How many wishes does Bobby have now?

27. Which came first in Ireland? The chicken or the egg?

28. What is brown-ish on the inside, is a symbol of the Emerald country, has a neck, but doesn't have a head?

29. What happens once in Ireland, once in English, twice in Haiti?

30. Although there are no female leprechauns, I am the queen of the shamrocks. I live in a commune, called a deck, with 51 others, as well as a couple of jokers. In my commune there are actually four kings, my husband and three others; the others rule over hearts, diamonds, and spades.

What is my name?

FUN FACT

Do you know what a Lobaircin is?
You'd be right, if you thought it
was a Leprechaun. This is the Irish
name for them, and it means
a 'small-bodied fellow.'

Chapter 3 - Answers

1. "Wrong". As a side note, you cannot say Irish people pronounce any word "wrongly" - they might do it in an Irish accent, but there's nothing wrong about it!

2. Not at all. Someone with a background in Irish lore would know there is no such thing as a female leprechaun; leprechauns are only male.

3. You used one wish by saying "Oh, how I wish I found you sooner!" which the leprechaun might not be able to materialize (because, despite his magic powers, he cannot bend time!) As such, you're only left with two.

4. The Leprechaun (who, to many people's surprise and amusement, is considered to be a fairy who makes shoes).

5. The Irish bouzoukis (which looks like a combination between a guitar and a mandolin). The name sounds like the combination between "buzz" and a Greek name, but this is a musical instrument the Irish take quite a lot of pride in.

6. Sign language (since billboards rely on mostly images to send across their messages).

7. Emerald. Although Ireland is quite rich in emeralds, most of the emeralds of the world come from Columbia.

8. The Emerald Island (which is what Ireland is sometimes called).

9. The Island of Ireland (where you will find Northern Ireland, which is part of the United Kingdom, and the Republic of Ireland, which is an independent country).

Chapter 3 - Answers

10. Literature. Ireland won the Nobel Prize for literature four times.

11. The Celtic Tiger (which is what Ireland was called at the end of the 1990s and beginning of the 2000s, as they were gaining quite a lot of economic power and transforming their country as a result).

12. The Gaelic language, one of the two official languages in Ireland (the other one being English).

13. The pot of gold at the end of the rainbow.

14. In the dictionary.

15. Mischief and trouble.

16. "March" (the month of St Patrick's)

17. The word "Irish" (it has two "i's" in it).

18. Thirteen (five in "Irish" and eight in "language").

19. Vikings (who attacked the Irish in the 9th century A.D.).

20. It would take twenty-two minutes for the leprechaun to microwave twenty-two servings of Irish stew (provided that they are the same size as the first 3 and that the same microwave is used, of course).

21. The map of Ireland.

22. 0; no one found any.

23. Kelly said he wasn't going to look any more; he didn't say he was going to look any less. ("Anymore" and "any more" mean two different things.)

Chapter 3 - Answers

24. Your nose will smell the best foods at St. Patrick's Day dinner.

25. The cauldron lid.

26. Three; he started with three - he used one and he gained one - so he still has three.

27. Theoretically, dinosaurs laid eggs long before chickens existed. Although only two dinosaur skeletons have been found in Ireland, it is fair to assume that they were not singular examples - and as such, it can be said that the egg came first (in Ireland and everywhere else, really).

28. A bottle of Guinness stout.

29. The letter "I".

30. The Queen of Clubs

Bonus Fun Facts
About Ireland
in Riddles

"I am a great believer in luck, and
I find the harder I work the more
I have of it"

~ Thomas Jefferson

Chapter 4 - Questions

1. If you delete one letter from this number, you get it all even. It's the number of times Ireland won the Eurovision contest!

What is the number?

2. Double the 50 and subtract two, with a little comma and two at the end, yoo-hoo! This is how many liters of beer an Irish person drinks in a year!

What is the number?

3. St. Patrick was not born in Ireland; he was born in me. Today I am part of the countries that comprise Great Britain. My name sounds like a chubby ocean mammal.

What am I?

4. We really like green, but one of our people designed the most famous house in the world.

What house is it?

5. Popular in Ireland, I have a meaning many don't know. I'm similar to a famous laptop brand, but I have nothing to show but stories about every Irish Joe.

Who am I?

FUN FACT

Would you want to kiss the Blarney Stone? This is an important part of Irish culture, it is believed that people who kiss it, become persuasive, articulate and expressive when they speak. It's not easy to kiss though! You have to go up to the top of Blarney Castle tower and lean backwards on the parapet's edge to kiss it. If you're scared of heights, it's not for you!

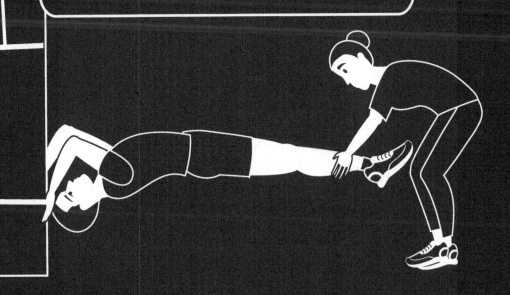

Chapter 4 - Questions

6. This equation if you solve, you get the height in meters of the third-highest cliff in Europe - Croaghaun, Ireland: (2*2*4*4-4)*10+90-2=?

7. Want to know why St. Patrick's Day is so popular way outside of the Irish borders? This number shows how many people around the world claim Irish heritage: 10*7*(3+4)=?

8. This trait has been associated with Irish mischief, but only about 10% here actually have it.
Hint: it's also one of the rarest chromatic qualities the human DNA can produce!

What trait is this?

9. I am the musical instrument that appears on both Irish and British coins. I have appeared on past flags of Ireland, and I am on the coat of arms of the Republic of Ireland, Canada, and the United Kingdom. You may think that I'm harping on about it, but I am a triangular instrument native to Scotland and Ireland.

What am I?

Chapter 4 - Questions

10. When he was 16, St. Patrick was captured by a group of us, people who ar-r-r-r-r-r. People associate us with the "R", but I am really fascinated with the seven C's. We showed the boy a jolly good time before selling him into slavery in Ireland, roger that.

Who are we?

11. I'm the only prime even number in the world - and the number of female presidents Ireland has had.

Who am I?

Chapter 4 - Questions

12. In this house, the lights are turned on when people go to sleep. If I don't get turned on, hundreds of people could die in the dark. I'm one of the oldest ones of my kind on the entire continent, and my name rhymes with "crook". Do you know who I am?

13. I am a reptile. I am long and limbless, but I can slither. I have no eyelids, but I do have a short tail. St, Patrick supposedly drove all my kind out of Ireland; doubters of his miraculous ability simply say my kind was never in Ireland in the first place because Ireland is so cold.

What am I?

14. Solve this math problem and you will learn the percentage of people under 28 currently living in Ireland! 3*(1+3+1)*3+1+3+1=...?

15. My name is very lively and I cut through Dublin in a continuous flow. Can you guess who I am?

16. They say I'm like a big fruit, and that I am the dreamer's pursuit. In the US I have the largest population of people claiming Irish ancestry.

What city am I?

17. We're known for St. Patrick's, but did you know we also invented the spookiest holiday in the world? Its name is...?

18. I was born in Ireland, I can live under the sea, but I'm fine on the surface too. I am not a magical creature.

What am I?

Chapter 4 - Questions

19. Solve this equation to learn the year in which the first yacht club in the world was founded in Cork Harbor, in Ireland! 2000-(3+9+10+110*2) =?

20. When leprechauns were first reported, they were not wearing clothes of green - they were wearing clothes of me. My name sounds as if you have pondered the ink marks on this page.

What color am I?

21. Our favorite fairy isn't a shoemaker for no reason! The Irish have invented a type of shoe that's made with rubber (but not entirely out of it), called...?

22. I am the original color of St. Patrick's Day celebrations; I am NOT green. Some people see me in the skies and think of optimism; other people think about me when they are sad. There is even a jazz-like music named for me.

What am I?

23. If you do not wear green on St. Patrick's Day, not only are you a party pooper but you will also likely experience people grabbing your flesh in between their finger and thumb while squeezing. Each person is only allowed to do this to you once. What is this act of grabbing flesh called?

FUN FACT

Do you know what traditional Irish dish is made from beef, potatoes, carrots and herbs? Irish Stew.

Chapter 4 - Questions

24. Multiply 5 by 10,000 and then subtract twice the multiplier to get the whole number of castles in Ireland! How many castles are there in Ireland?

25. We take our fairies quite seriously, you see! If you add 2 and 2 and multiply by 2 to add another 2, you will get the number of years we've delayed building a motorway to protect a tree that belonged to our beloved fairies! How many years is that?

26. What do the Statue of Liberty, The Empire State Building, Niagara Falls, several landmarks in Cannes, France, the Dusseldorf Lighthouse, and the Sydney Opera House have in common every March?

27. If you multiply 3 by 30, multiply 2 by 4, and pull them together, you'll get the shortest St. Patrick's Day parade ever! How short is it?

28. Double 1,000, then subtract 30 and add 1 three times. This is when Ireland joined the European Union! When was this?

29. Did you know St. Patrick's is an official holiday in just two places on Earth? One is (obviously!) Ireland, and the other one means "serrated mountain" and it is located in the Caribbean. Can you guess its name?

Chapter 4 - Questions

30. After St. Patrick was sold into slavery, his master placed him in charge of guarding these animals. Wolves and other creatures were all too willing to eat both St. Patrick and the wool-bearing creatures he was tending. Ironically, when St. Patrick later worked in churches, people still said he tended these creatures? What is the name of these animals?

31. I'm similar to the name of an area, a continent, and the official currency of Ireland.

What am I?

Chapter 4 - Questions

32. I am a large metal pot, typically made of cast iron, usually black in color, commonly used for cooking over an open fire. Leprechauns, though, use me to store their gold coins. Some people say that I am called Ron, but I will answer to any name you give me.

What am I?

33. If you do 4+3+2+1*3-1, you will get the age at which St. Patrick is believed to have been enslaved. What was the age?

34. In football, this country's all white and blue, but one day a year, they turn into green, for true! In fact, they hold the largest St. Patrick's celebrations in South America, mind you! Can you guess who they are, who?

35. Take 2 out of 10, multiply by 2, and then add 2 and another 2. That's Ireland's place in the list of the largest islands in the world! How big an island is Ireland?

36. The Atlantic Ocean, Its Superbly Emerald Chants and History. Take "and" from this sentence, then grab each initial letter - that's how the Irish Prime Minister is officially called!

What is the name?

Chapter 4 - Questions

37. I am a three-leafed plant; if you find a fourth leaf on one of my kind, you are considered lucky. I am also the national symbol of Ireland. St. Patrick used me to teach about the Holy Trinity.

What am I?

38. At the age of 26, St. Patrick ran away from his slave master and successfully boarded a boat bound for England. He returned to England and sought refuge in a place full of monks. The monks that lived there gave him chants as well as chances. Where did St. Patrick go?

39. The leprechaun knows a nine-letter word that can hold hundreds of letters.

What is it?

40. Add 2 to 20 and twice 450, sum it all up with 1,000 - this is when Ireland won its independence from Great Britain! When did this happen?

41. Two multiplied by two twice, and then the result multiplied again by two - this is how many counties you'll find on the Irish island! How many are there?

FUN FACT

Do you know what Lá Fhéile Pádraig means? It's Irish for St. Patrick's Day and means 'the Day of the Festival of Patrick'.

Lá Fhéile Pádraig

Chapter 4 - Questions

42. The shamrock's no happenstance mind you! In fact, each of the clover's leaves represents something: one stands for a synonym of belief, the other one stands for what you feel when you really want Santa to bring you what you wanted, and the other one stands for the fuzziest and warmest feeling in the world. Can you guess what these are?

---

43. What do Google, PayPal, Twitter, and Apple have in common, other than the fact that they are all tech companies? Can you guess?

---

44. Whenever people in the movies scream "Clear!" in a medical context, they're using me, but what they don't know is my origins are Irish.

What am I?

---

45. I rhyme with the wig, but I don't sit on the head. In fact, I'm more about the feet than anything else. They call me the Irish...?

---

46. Take the letters associated with each of these numbers, bring them together, and you will get a type of Irish pancake: 2, 15, 24, 20, 25.

What is its name?

Chapter 4 - Questions

47. They say I'm small enough to sit on your shoulder, but my fairy-given powers can move mountains and I have a lot of gold. I bet you already know who I am!

Who am I?

48. Subtract eight out of ten and add two, then subtract one and double it, will you? This is the number of counties you'll find in Northern Ireland! How many counties are there in Northern Ireland?

Chapter 4 - Questions

49. Double 200 and then double again, subtract two quarters out of it and you're set: this is the minimum number of international places that go green on St.Patrick's Day. How many are there?

50. Green is our flag, green is our pride, over the hills and across the mountainside, over the ocean and the entire world, we rule through greenness and a big old hug!

Who are we?

Chapter 4 - Answers

1. 7 (Eurovision, 2020)

2. 98.2 (Smith, 2018)

3. Wales

4. The White House, which was designed by James Hoban (Wikipedia, 2020)

5. "Mac" (a prefix frequently encountered in Irish family names, which means "son of", just like "O'" means "grandson of") (Britannica, 2020).

6. 688 (Wikipedia, 2020).

---

7. 70 million (Haynie, 2016).

8. Red hair (March 2017)

9. Celtic Harp

10. Pirates

11. Two (Wilde,2019)

12. The Hook Lighthouse (Wikipedia, 2020)

13. Snake

14. 50.(Irish Around the World, 2019)

15. River Liffey

16. New York (Wikipedia, 2020)

17. Halloween (CladdaghDesighn, 2017)

18. Submarine (Wikipedia, 2020)

19. 1770 (ASA, 2020)

---

20. Red

21. Rubber sole shoe (Bellis, 2019)

22. Blue (Esposito, 2015)

23. Pinching

24. 30,000 (Enjoy-Irish-Culture, 2020)

25. 10 (SoundsofSirius, 2020)

26. They all light up in green on St.Patrick's Day!

27. 98 feet (HotSprings, 2020)

28. 1973 (Europa.eu, 2020)

29. Montserrat (TheJournal, 2016)

30. Sheep

31. Euro

Chapter 4 - Answers

32. Cauldron

33. 16 (Wikipedia, 2020)

34. Argentina (Wander-Argentina, 2020)

35. 20 (Wikipedia, 2020)

36. Taoiseach

37. A Shamrock

38. A monastery

39. A letterbox.

40. 1922 (Wikipedia, 2020)

41. 32 (WesleyJohnston, 2020).

42. Faith, hope, love.

43. They all have their European HQ in Ireland

---

44. Mobile defibrillator (Wikipedia, 2020)

45. The Irish Jig (a type of tap-dancing in traditional Irish folklore)

46. Boxty

47. Leprechaun

48. 6 (WesleyJohnston, 2020)

49. 400 (BBC,2019)

50. The IRISH!

Did you enjoy the book?

If you did, we are ecstatic. If not, please write your complaint to us and we will ensure we fix it.

If you're feeling generous, there is something important that you can help me with – tell other people that you enjoyed the book.

Ask a grown-up to write about it on Amazon. When they do, more people will find out about the book. It also lets Amazon know that we are making kids around the world laugh. Even a few words and ratings would go a long way.

If you have any ideas or jokes that you think are super funny, please let us know. We would love to hear from you. Our email address is -

riddleland@riddlelandforkids.com

Riddleland Bonus Book

Join our **Facebook Group** at **Riddleland for Kids** to get daily jokes and riddles.

Bonus Book

https://pixelfy.me/riddlelandbonus

Thank you for buying this book. As a token of our appreciation, we would like to offer a special bonus—a collection of 50 original jokes, riddles, and funny stories.

CONTEST

Would you like your jokes and riddles to be featured in our next book?

We are having a contest to discover the cleverest and funniest boys and girls in the world!

1) Creative and Challenging Riddles
2) Tickle Your Funny Bone Contest

Parents, please email us your child's "original" riddle or joke. **He or she could win a $25 Amazon gift card and be featured in our next book.**

Here are the rules:

1) We're looking for super challenging riddles and extra funny jokes.

2) Jokes and riddles MUST be 100% original—NOT something discovered on the Internet.

3) You can submit both a joke and a riddle because they are two separate contests.

4) Don't get help from your parents—UNLESS they're as funny as you are.

5) Winners will be announced via email or our Facebook group – Riddleland for Kids.

6) In your entry, please confirm which book you purchased.

Email us at <u>Riddleland@riddlelandforkids.com</u>

Other Fun Books by Riddleland
Riddles Series

FUN
RIDDLES
AND TRICK QUESTIONS
FOR KIDS AND FAMILY!

300 RIDDLES AND BRAIN TEASERS THAT
KIDS AND FAMILY WILL ENJOY

CREATIVE
RIDDLES
AND TRICK QUESTIONS
FOR KIDS AND FAMILY!

300 RIDDLES AND BRAIN TEASERS THAT
KIDS AND FAMILY WILL ENJOY

AWESOME
RIDDLES
AND TRICK QUESTIONS
FOR KIDS

300 FUN BRAIN-STUMPERS
FOR AGES 9 TO 12

RIDDLELAND

AWESOME
RIDDLES
AND TRICK QUESTIONS
FOR KIDS

PUZZLING QUESTIONS AND FUN FACTS
FOR AGES 5 TO 8

FUN HALLOWEEN
RIDDLES
AND TRICK QUESTIONS
FOR KIDS AND FAMILY!

300 RIDDLES AND BRAIN TEASERS THAT
KIDS AND FAMILY WILL ENJOY

FUN
THANKSGIVING
RIDDLES
AND TRICK QUESTIONS
FOR KIDS AND FAMILY!

300 RIDDLES AND BRAIN TEASERS THAT
KIDS AND FAMILY WILL ENJOY

RIDDLELAND

RIDDLELAND

FUN
CHRISTMAS
RIDDLES
AND TRICK QUESTIONS
FOR KIDS AND FAMILY!

300 RIDDLES AND BRAIN TEASERS THAT
KIDS AND FAMILY WILL ENJOY

RIDDLELAND

The Laugh Challenge Joke Series

Would You Rather Series

Get them on Amazon or our website at
www.riddlelandforkids.com

About Riddleland

Riddleland is a mum and dad run publishing company. We are passionate about creating fun and innovative books to help children develop their reading skills and fall in love with reading. If you have suggestions for us or want to work with us, shoot us an email at

riddleland@riddlelandforkids.com

Our family's favorite quote

"Creativity is an area in which younger people have a tremendous advantage since they have an endearing habit of always questioning past wisdom and authority."

– Bill Hewlett.

Made in the USA
Las Vegas, NV
11 March 2023